MW01673419

Karma's Capricious Land and Other Poems of Love and Dissolution

Indira Umareddy

PARTRIDGE

Copyright © 2023 by Indira Umareddy.

ISBN:	Hardcover	978-1-5437-7056-8
	Softcover	978-1-5437-7054-4
	eBook	978-1-5437-7055-1

All rights reserved. No part of this book may be used or reproduced by any means, graphic, electronic, or mechanical, including photocopying, recording, taping or by any information storage retrieval system without the written permission of the author except in the case of brief quotations embodied in critical articles and reviews.

Because of the dynamic nature of the Internet, any web addresses or links contained in this book may have changed since publication and may no longer be valid. The views expressed in this work are solely those of the author and do not necessarily reflect the views of the publisher, and the publisher hereby disclaims any responsibility for them.

Photo Credit: Biju Nair

Print information available on the last page.

To order additional copies of this book, contact
Toll Free +65 3165 7531 (Singapore)
Toll Free +60 3 3099 4412 (Malaysia)
orders.singapore@partridgepublishing.com

www.partridgepublishing.com/singapore

Contents

Falling in Love

Shades of Love

The Parting

The Calm After

Of Ancient Tales

Falling in Love

Love

Love, beyond-lifetimes love,
tiny-little-sweet-childhood love,
kitchen-heat-sweat ruined-meal love
Menial love, transactional love,
a lonely night's-lustful love,
ritual-filial-brotherly love,
tea-time-tenderness-love,
tracking flight-path-nervous love,
saree-end-clumping-touchy love,
hand-shake-is-enough-too love
White-sheet-wrapped-up-nude-love
Here, hold my hand and stand up to love

What if life slipped its tangled mess on our feet and got ahead?
Maybe then, skip the race, don't catch up, clean up, just be?
Cushioned by the delicious mess,
here hold my hand and dwell here a while

Broken-bitter love, pupil-dilating,
heart-rate-pumping love
Dazzling firework-love, oil-mud-lamp-love
Burning, shining, crazy, flaming love
Whichever way you find love,
here, hold my hand and stand up to love
Pointless love

Under purple skies behind the horizon
Dawn met the dusk in moments lapsing before their birth: you met me
They told me that our space is a deep, dark, noiseless ocean
and the blue God is cushioned by a coiled snake
And love, little love, the pointless torch.

Falling

Does a caterpillar know
She is to be a butterfly?
And still, she goes fearlessly
into a deep dark cave with
perhaps no tomorrow.

Who Has Time for the Stars?

We came clenching our unformed fists into fate lines.
I held up my palm against yours, willing it to entwine
drum rolls, shivers in the spine, golden autumn rays,
scars on your skin—all sing in unheard tuneless ways.
But what about those dark spaces in our music?

At a distance, I crave a two-syllabled sweet moon,
Raindrop-pitched murmurs on a long-lost parched tune,
Your skin that erupts in a million smiles at my touch,
dark oval moles spewing perfumes of earth, and such.
But would you look up from your mirror?

In silence, I watch the moon drape a saree of light,
which her stealthy sun sent through his secret sprite.
She danced with twenty-seven stars, each night anew,
And here and now waits for a lone glimpse of you.
But who has time for the stars?

Come Walk with Me

Come walk with me and hold my hand.
I will meet you at the nook where history takes a turn.
Do you remember that long journey out of the place we called home?
I carry memories of that migration in my viscera.
They say some can peer down the microscope and trace your roots.

I can smell that in your embrace;
that fragrant forest clearing, warmth of bonfire and
the starriest night before the dawn of humankind.
I walked with you and held your hand
as we entered this world of myriad possibilities.

Come walk with me and hold my hand.
Those hoary rituals of life and death, music of a bygone era,
pressed flowers of precious nothings—
each of these is born again in you and me.
Yes, they are, every single day.
I can see them all each time I look into your eyes.

Come walk with me and hold my hand.
Gathering precious memories in my hand,
let me count these pebbles on the seashore of lapsed time.
Let me breathe life into lost moments
when I taste your skin again.

Come walk with me and hold my hand.
Do not turn away from that black hole of the future:
don't you know of the wormhole of memory?
It will bring us back—the very DNA that set us on this path.

My Very Own

To all those choices you will make
in those moments of closed eyes
and clenched fists that overwhelm you,
steady you, or trip you over,

my daughter, you who are my very own
and yet not quite,
this ache in my heart
is for all that and more.

The day first saw you
through an enchanted lens of science and faith,
we peered into my womb
and caught you sucking your thumb.

That sterile room came alive—
a sweeping vision of awe, fear, and bliss.
I wondered then if I had ever known love
before I stepped into that room.

I bowed then to life, to death, and rebirth,
to my mother who had foreseen this for me,
and to your daughter who will too.
But from that moment, my daughter,
you have been my very own but not quite.

This ache in my heart is for those choices you will make,
all those moments of closed eyes and clenched fists
that will overwhelm you, steady you, or trip you over—
for all that and much more.

How to Kiss Your Dream

At first, you struggle, and then he fumbles:
wetness meets warmth, wilderness tumbles
behind closed doors of yesteryear's failings.
You lock your arms around moonlit railings;
when breath meets skin, a magical mark appears.
Lips dissolve into lips, and the world disappears,
and then you come up for air as if you'd drown.
But blessings are being handed on lust's crown
Wine, vodka, wonky voodoo watery wishes
Hand out a handy mix to yield to death's wanton kisses.
And that's how, dear life,
You kiss a dream: on his full cotton lips.

Poetry

Wordy kaleidoscopes
into that otherworldly
dusk-light, tributes to
a jasmine-haunted
lucent late evening,

our now-Cimmerian
story just being poured
out letter by letter as though
by a poet from the clouds,

poetry is that purple saree
hanging from our ceiling
fan; yes, that same one sold
faulty by a thrice-greedy

salesman in the shop, whose
name sometimes flashes
into my mind at random
prompts by jasmine
notes in brightly lit malls,
dimly lit temples, terrible
purple hues of party
balloons—poetry is those

sadly tangled syllables,
anklets round your feet
I held on to while a
purple knot on your neck

remained lodged in my words,
these needless pages,
and all the holes that I ever
dug to bury all the whys.

Poetry is the question from my
lost childhood, silent alliterations
to silence wordless whispers
in the wind.

If I were good enough—for you,
for us, and for all the poets
known and unknown—would
kaleidoscopes still be a deep purple?

Shades of Love

Call Me by My Name Again

Night after night of restless joy,
day after day of utter despair,
feigned apathy and nerves wait on

a thousand questions unanswered,
a single word that says it all,
those jumps and starts,
narrations of someone else's past;

untouched food, my glass you took,
those spasms of fear,
bouts of brazen desire,
one rainy afternoon and a drenched night—
to make you call me by my name again, what would it take?

Double Cross

Love me as you would love a woman;
no child, no whore, no mother am I,
just a double cross on your single Y.
Can I hold a kiss and never let go?
Build temples and worship your toes?
Live every day as if it were the last,
each moment with you as if the first?

So love me as you would love a woman;
no god, no dog, nor the ocean's blue.
I am a two-faced bitch—it's true, it is.
Turn me around, and you will find
a saint that's right and a sinner without bound.

I seek in you what you seek of me:
the missing part that was made not to fit;
lightness, laughter, limericks, and all
life's unbound charm; its deep chasms for free fall,
open winds, open wounds, closed to the world
on cloudy days and rainy nights.

I seek of you what you see in me.
Do love me as a woman: I am
but a double cross on your single Y.

Alive

They are alive, those moments
Fogging my multicoloured mirrors of memory
With their sweet, effervescent breath,
smooth and stark, bittersweet
in that pain of pleasure,
a hint of red, a hint of blue
forever swirling in the kaleidoscope
of renewal of desire and death.
And here at once they converge
into your image, those moments
holding my hand and its brush
splashing rainbow sprinkles,
snowflakes, rose petals—
oh, the sheer colour of life!
They are alive in my breath,
those moments,
and in every word you write.
If they seem embalmed
in amber, do not be sad,
dear love:
they are throbbing inside with
a life that can be renewed in
a jiffy. Come, all it takes is your word,
and they are alive,
those moments.

Sit by Me

Your moonlit form in shadows
tinged every poem written in prose,
memories of all my good times,
all open spaces, all dearest faces,

and now you are here,
and now I hold your hand,
no rimeless fear mars
now this timeless rebirth

of our beloved evening star.
Yes, when the morning arrives,
no shadows will breathe,
and neither Venus nor the moon

or I will run once again
in search of your precious,
scented breath in a random
page filled with delicious words.

Then you write in many tongues of
history, of war, and of human desire, of
what needs to be said and said over again
to be known, that to be loved is to be born again.

Staying Sane

Twenty-one reasons to remain
attractive at forty-two:
two children, a home in all shades of blue,
cars, cards, cuddles, and the sweet pain

of knowing that each night at nine, we kiss
and tiny, timid polka dots light up the sky;
perfect porcelain angels look on, do not fly,
handing out stabbing aches called bliss.

I wonder if you know that I am sane now,
attractive at forty-two, two lifetimes
into these Marie Kondo shelves, glorious primes,
rid of your insane breath, sober, and how!

Chinnu, Before You Taught Me to Love

I was to teach you the ways of this world.
How does one conjure jungles and jinns?
When to let rainbows pour onto lilac walls?
Where can you skip, hop, and land
in moody monsoon's muddy puddles?

Who to cling to when bubbles, balloons,
all the bells and all the balls are gone?
Why do stars twinkle and not ceiling lights?
Which sand knob on the beach turns
the snow-white sliver-moon on?
All night I look up the best ways to
Teach: Google, YouTube, gurus, gods,
but no books—

no books taught me how to braid
peacock feathers, yards of jasmine
into tender coconut fronds,
as Siri paints a myriad of pandemics
on a mute pink rash on your freckled arm.

Strangers, and their dangerous gaits—
Mothers say I should
teach you of the world at large,
but for one more day, another hour, dear daughter,
ere: learn to hold my hand and reach
for the ocean waves in those monsoon puddles.

Prefect's Towel

(An Ode to the Hitchhiker's guide to the Galaxy)

Grab these cheat sheets to 42 with or without a loved one.
Smear on galaxial highways a dense yellow sheen
of spinning yarns, of ripening, of having been, of not being done …

Towels! Yes, towels! Beach towels,
bath towels, hand towels,
kitchen towels, face towels,
sweet-scented paper towels;

lush collective pinnacles of human effects
in faded ice-cream pastels, royal ivory, or intrepid Madras checks,
raw bruised cottons, soft PVA viscose, or Turkish luxury pecks;

towels to dry the boobs, towels to hide the tears,
Towels to furl the sails, towels to fold the fears,
towels and more towels to wipe away bottomless years …

take twenty towels in white and two in pink.
Count infinite galaxies as one in a soul-sink.
Repeat, rinse; repeat, and do not panic.

2020

Twenty odd years into the century,
with strange happenings in all
corners of a pale blue dot,
it was said that hearts frozen
in loneliness blow up dead stars
as well as they could men,
women, and children—

all it took was a cocktail of
snowflakes and ancient uranium,

or maybe it was a myth
from many years before
when watchmakers were yet
to melt needles into backlit digits,

when all those spaces
between words could be painted
into pages of a stranger's thoughts—
a nuance, a comma, the way one
goes about collecting snowflakes—
sitting on the equator peering into
instant faces, hashtags, storylines,
distant galaxies of other people's worlds.

Twenty odd years into the century,
with strange happenings in all
corners of a pale blue dot,
there is no room

to remember differently from you
those shades of an afternoon spent
in the rain,
frozen forever
into filtered pictures of fun

So no—not even one of these
seven billion jailed by a tiny thread
of nucleic acids will find the will
to swim, to implode, or to search

for another star, another flight, another
way to hug families now fully aware
that the famed vastness of oceans
is no longer a myth,

Bit by bit, before the snowflakes
settle, we dig the earth for another
hour, another way to spend the year
and send a camera-craft to Mars for uranium.

Go

Be gone, words,
You easy sluts
you come and go
as you wish
I wish no more
for your charmed light,
you friendly butterflies,
alphabet symphonies.
be gone, you pretenders,
unloving mothers
of my stillborn thoughts.
Don't buzz, don't swirl, do not
come one by one and silently
stand at the cobwebbed corners
of my still-less mind.
Your silence is a hoax,
a web of quantum tangles,
one syllable here and another
echo somewhere down
memory maps on the dark side
of the moon. But there you go
again, you words, you weird
masters of my destiny—
I speak no more of you.
Pray, leave, be gone,
you words.
Go measure the ends of this
universe in your lengthy,
pithy tales—
one hand, one pair of lips,
one wandering lock of hair,

every minute that I ever
lived now locked in your
cruel jails. Go! Leave, words, and
let me be.
Go, leave now, and let there be me.

Pandemic Tales

An ocean welled up to
wipe away these words.
No angels with or without wings
could stand by while
drop by drop the ocean swelled
into a primordial inferno
and then just so surely
dried itself up.

Surely, those words remain etched
in mismatched memories of hurt
and regret, swirling around
as dust storms must do in deserts.

If I could take away every
moment when your hand was not
in mine, surely I would rewrite our
story again. But of what use is
yet another story of loss in a world
torn apart by a tiny capsule of
a virus, neglect, miscalculation,
panic, greed, and—who knows—
Maybe even nobility?
Surely all
the sentinels of faith would write
new stories of hope and love
when all this is over.

And again, while the angels sleep,
on moonlit nights, long dark roads,
bridges, skywalks, a corridor of white
spaces, eternity, with my feet on yours
holding on to dear life, surely I would
fashion a wormhole
to connect yearning and regret;
if not a wormhole, why not
elevators, airplanes, your doorstep,
one hundred coffees,
and those letters
we neither wrote nor read.

Surely I will write about that
broken past, blocked but only a door
away. Or a phone call, a message,
unspoken anger in unwritten texts,
blank calls. Imagined lovers.
Voluntary blessings. Partings,
another day, another life, without
you, without me, with many
what-ifs and could-have-beens
with the others that had left our
mutually empty lives before we began.

But the ocean that was to come
between us is so far away. Now
there is no way to make friends
with distance and lockdowns.
Surely we have masks and taxis
and a possibility to wipe away
everything that ever began?
One day when we stop
being the pandemic people,
surely our story
will be written fresh
on stars borne again by
angels with or without wings,
and surely those hands will
hold on to one another, even if
there was a tomorrow.

Staircase to Stars

Under this umbrella lie all the stars.
Hold out your palm to the open skies.
Pins and needles—nay, gallons of pain—
twists and turns, and a wrenching of hearts,

all will be well with this blueprint of love,
when my fingertips write on your naked wrist.
All will be well with poets and songs,
once you reclaim our nook from those books.

Love asked me if I believe, and I laughed once
and was, stripped of skin and again of blood,
I write these tales of white truth and dark lies,
on pages and pages of unfounded myths

that in all those people I was to love
was hidden a mirror, an endless nadir.
Again and again with hope, with despair,
I search in your eyes that staircase to stars.

An Affair

Right is never wrong, and so it goes,
but once it's said so,
the right to say "I love you"
is altogether and entirely wronged.

At a time and place when all wrongs
felt out of place, you and I
threw fistfuls of gilded memories at
bottomless wells of why-nots.

Today I tried to swim there,
but my limbs forgot to move.
My left leg tripped on yours,
only nothing seemed right.

Alone I travelled to the star
which we once named with
joined finger trails, up there, above,
the ladder that stayed but the sky was wrong.

You and I, have no right,
no sky, well, land on earth where
left and right feel altogether
and entirely wrong.

And yet
wrong is never right,
and so it goes
once it's said so.

Kintsugi

Words tore us apart just as they
had brought us together. No eyes,
no skin, no lips, no sensual breath
sucking in all of our scattered lives
into a white hole of hands held on
dark, unending starlit nights
could restrain those floods of
clamorous, cruel, crushing words—
my words, your words, our needless words,
now broken and scattered
words.
I plead and I pray to gods
of the past, present and of pain
to never make me whole again
without a golden seam of this
beautiful mess running through
each drop of blood in my veins,
my very spine,
eyes, skin, lips, and sensual breath.
Who knows, maybe with each curve
filled with crumbling words,
all my straight lines will at last
tumble and fall through these
remaining cracks in my soul,
and what would remain then
is a darkened seam. No words
will regret, having ever been
broken. And I will be whole again.

Beetles

Old thoughts, like resin-embedded beetles,
lie around in double blue-ticked boxes;
some white, some green, all certainly dead,
throbbing with possibilities of a time
when white fury lashed out on two sides
of an unspoken, wordy fight
or of lust-shaped emojis of tender joy.
Some asked for attention;
a few showered praises.
It was clear that the beetles led
different lives at different times.
But here they lie staring into time,
all of a same colour of a past undone.

Fani, the Cyclone

I saw him hurrying past me,
devouring the sky and its land
in a darkness born
to that fecund womb
of beginnings and endings—
they said he was fate.

But I knew that
no one asked him if
his mouth bled from
osseous remains
of his fated meals,

and I knew
that he hid from
swirling singing
Clouds, from death,
and mostly from wind.

I saw him crash into
safe roofs, sound walls,
violent floors of what were
once homes, drunk on
desperate dirges.

Far away from his home
in that yonder ocean's
depths, he died alone,
somewhere inland,
smaller than he ever was.

They said by that time,
not a leaf trembled
at his touch.

Straight from my lips

My love is selfish.
My love hates you too.
On days like this, it takes the
form of a nebulous cloud
and thunders on about eternity
while sprinkling throughout
long evenings of loss a sense
of having been home, once.
My love is pretty, ugly, angry.
Sweet notes of separation
mingle with your sweat all of a sudden,
and then torrents of
unconsummated lifetimes flow
your blood into my cells,
your breath in my silent womb.
My love is a stain
of vermillion on your hand,
straight from my lips—
and who knows from
what pushes and pulls
that the forlorn moon has
cast upon those timely tides.
Languid, lustrous, gorgeous moon,
forever a mirror to another's
scarred light,
Searching star-strewn streets
for a tiny black hole that will hold
all of its lies, tears, and its entire mouth.

Second Kiss

Round and round
on this merry-go-round,
we go on and on spinning yarns
of pleasure and pain into pleats
of my saree. But when we get
to unveil this fabric of guilt,
you take a step back, and so do I.
We can run away from each other,
like those galaxies
they say one day all will crash
into one,
until I collapse in your exhausted arms
and ask if ever we had a beginning,
if ever a second time we kissed.

Steady

Love is a word, an image,
sweetness and solitude,
sticky-sweet cotton candy,
that never quite begins until it ends,

lingers on the tongue,
and writes slow shivers across
memories whose nerves
have never quite unwound.

But maybe it is that broken glass
stuck in my feet
while mopping your floor;

a light-hearted remark,
implying that faith, forever
gone, was once full.

Other days, I drink to life,
but on days like this
I drink to love and say
love is a fidgeting child

who on leisurely afternoons
elopes with you beyond the hills;
other days, he sulks in a corner,

and I sit with him.
I caress his stories
And say love is time
lost, found, and simply known.

Fairy Tales

Allow me to write it all up:
farmyard tales of
not-for-any-reason blues.
Once princes were made
of men in horses who
wrung a parrot's neck to meet
their women.
Shiny, glitzy tales, sturdy folksy tales,
swords and wits and battles to be won,
stars to be strung on a night's lustful yarn—
the books wind themselves up
after being read, make themselves
a cup of tea, and wait
for another human to reach another world,
a different-coloured country,
a darker-hued woman.
Allow me to turn this page again
and see if the yellowed letters
stole some stardust
from a long-ago night
on that very bridge.

Seagulls

All of us seagulls lined up
next to one another, our togetherness
measured in metres.
A few million years ago,
when moonlit nights were unwitnessed,
all men and all women
unborn were seeking
that one song, that one line, that one glance—
Too far away from one's soul,
too close to where one belongs—
and then these eyes were made.
So they search for another or
for that perfect answer to empty spaces
and baby universes
creeping out of wormholes all around
like seagulls.
No one came with a coffee cup
and a book to curl up with to say,
"If you want my life, come and take it,"
and no one saw those seagulls scatter.

Sorted Desire

How do we sort desire?
This one is proper; the other, shallow.
This goes into the blue box of pursuit,
that one into the red box of next week;
these go into the pale pink box of never-go-there.

There must be rooms full of the unfulfilled desires
of various women somewhere
on our planet,
breathing in nicotine fumes of
memories soaked in regret,
and boatfuls of children's winged desires
of spaceman spiffs atop Attenborough's
predator cats deep inside a sphinx's hollow.

Men must have their trains and buses full, too,
Of things they once desired, withered
in the vacuity of repetition and
cookie-cutter travel maps, hotels, malls.
Ocean dives, gliders, northern lights
Not as enticing as in travel vlogs.

And when tiny desires are fulfilled—
a kiss from behind, feet lifted off the ground
in faint, dizzy aftermath of slow lovemaking—
they fall off the face of earth and float
around like stars, expanding into multiverses
Or maybe they float on radio waves, captured
aeons later by men and by women
into coloured boxes of desire

To Die Again

We write of children, wars, and books
as though the world is made up
of naked waters off sandless shores.

Together, four arms bring into this earth
a space that has been carved in heaven
we love and we love again—

and yet we speak of jobs,
green papers, losses and gains.

When he was born, he knew
and so Cupid remained
this dear dwarf on hoary walls,

while love failed again and again
to come out into real life
from frescos, stardust, memories, lust.

of wars we write when we think
of courage,
not of the deathly
desire to love
yet again.

Beauty's Black Spot

So busy was I arranging my joy
into bouquets of memories,

those red kisses overlaid
with white sprays of hope,
star-spangled afternoons

entwined in arms, legs, hair,
breaths, blankets, bites and all,

that I forgot to draw a black dot
on treasured touches to
ward off time's inevitable eye.

Will You?

I will walk with you down those hills
as the shadow follows its sunlit self
across those untouched desert sands,
places named after sounds and winds.
Will you follow footsteps of tomorrow?

I will be in the starlight that you seek
at a full moon dusk, half-lit, half-drowned,
at an ocean that churned without remorse
and gently curved your fate lines into mine.
Will you set your palm upon mine?

I will wait for you near our river at the alcove
a hundred years ago, a million years from now;
you parted my hair and painted scarlet kisses
and brought me sarees woven of cardamom scents.
Will you tie those jasmine dreams in my hair?

I will be the name that you will close your eyes to
as cold water touches your face in naked spaces.

Origins

I have no origins, no beginnings and endings;
at least, I remember none, except maybe

anxious Diwali evenings spent waiting for
my glorious, lonesome Amma's scooter to
be parked where it belonged,

flooded streets on monsoon afternoons,
holding hands with a little one who thought
I knew our way back home,

a cyclone that could have eliminated
a bus full of sixteen-year-old dreams for a world
they'd live to never find,

and that much-awaited first flight to a colder land
filling pages with loneliness, an unnamed passion
that never stopped yearning,

hands held after tears dried up
into easy compromises, smooth evenings,
long afternoons of sad songs on loop—

maybe the beginning was as in movies
from Russia, something as pointless
as fingers pointing together to a red star.

Your Story

Your stories are all silent movies of yore,
painted in every shade of white and grey.

In the hushed hours between wakefulness,
jump, start, loop, and return to where
everything is only just beginning.
And you, the hero of every book I ever read,

at that turn when your story met mine,
they say night jasmines bloom to this day.

Telugu Song

There we sang our love song,
twins bound by destiny,
both resting our heads on arms
of life, dear life, as precious
as paramecium, amoeba,
redwood trees, Brahminy kites.

Therein we sowed
lies that kept us alive,
water, air, that deep blue
sky, all but real—a screen
perhaps for what lies
deep inside you and me.

Then they sent us to earth.
But when we fell from those stars,
your flesh was made in another's
womb. My heart beat to a strange
rhythm. In time, screens and frames
made me a different you.

Our forgotten song, smudged
by stardust, buried in oceans' roar,
caroused through my veins, your
nerves. A stranger's sigh, another's
nimble limbs: all these and more
echoes of a past that screamed to live.

One afternoon,
one evening,
and one full night,
dear twin, we hummed
that sweet Telugu song:
Lo, we were alive …

Wounds

I drape a hundred lights on scabs of gloom
and dance around words, flights, dinners,
Blurred faces, wide smiles, crinkled eyes.
Not a drop of rain, not a word of you,
but at night, I stare at that sky, dark
as hell, with its zillions of burning wounds.

Another Dream

On lonely roads, I yearn for untainted moments, desire unquelled,
sitting face to face with an unexpressed wish to be held.

Pink umbrella, bitter coffee, passion fruit macaroons,
monsoon clouds, loneliness and unfulfilled boons—

such a short story, this tale of your life and mine together:
hands held but briefly, skin to nerves, an affair of the weather.

I hold up muddled monsoon mirrors to my soul and ask
if skin makes love to the heart, or does it wear a mask?

I douse my skin every night and dawn in jasmine, neroli, and rose.
What's washed still lingers, and your scent on my soul flows.

Oh, to draw short stories into a multilayered tome,
resting my skin on your soul's sweet home!

Your Image

When the stars fade away, our breaths will remain,
as vapour clouds herald a great summer rain,
perhaps my hand will reach out to the great void
and touch your voice from behind those clouds.

I swear to you that I did know it was your skin,
your lonesome eyes, and your hungry embrace
in all that darkness which was in my mother's womb,
and your sweet smile, the last image I'd ever see.

Belt Up

Belt up, buck up, shut up, and let's go
on such a long road to finding pieces
to glue together.
Yes, words shatter souls,
hearts lay in dust of scorn,
contempt and malice
overwhelm what once was
tender touch of lust.
So too cities were razed to dust,
stories were lost to history,
and yet blood flows downwards,
sky is filled with dawns and dusks
of impartial punctuality,
and you and I breathe.
So come on, let's go
find what pieces we can
of our lost selves, glue them
together.
If a mangled piece of me
gets strangled in your going-forward
step, I will be blessed.
So let me belt up.

Obsession

Obsession is my new middle name.
There were days, nay, years that passed
with my not knowing bacteria from a boson,
and decades of learning of the dance
within of receptors, proteins folding up,
unfolding, snapping and latching,
moving cells, life, blood, eyes, your
deep grey pools, no different from mine,
and yet, in all that's within, as different
as a bacterium to a boson.
I obsess these days on meanings,
on words said not meant,
on feelings that were once alive
and throbbed under a heart that beat
all its lifetimes' beats in those seconds
when you held my hand in worship
of the one force of nature that is alive
in your dance and mine together.
I obsess on the word *together*,
alone and never apart, together and
so separate, blood mingled once,
and yet leading us on distant forked
paths of half-alive memories of
moonlight, stardust, yellow orioles,
hundreds of steps together—now
together no longer. Obsessed.
No longer.

Tiny Love

Ambling along in an unguarded agora,
I closed my palm tight on my tiny love
and gazed at all that I wanted for now.

Dear love, you broken magnificent gem
which wasn't enough for a lifetime together,
they said you would buy me regret forever.

That Very Sun

The moon had always chased the sun,
strapped as it were to earth's gravity,

but all its sighs do is
pull on heartstrings of lunatics

far beneath the clouds
that they wished to climb.

Those clouds, they wish too
for moonless, star-drenched nights

where twin souls go to make love
on numbered nights of togetherness

and ages later smell each other's lips
in first rains drenching the ground

while the moon pursues her fortnightly
death, her undying desire for that very sun.

Write Me a Poem

You say I am a woman made of dreams,
blood, nerves, hormones, a dark womb.
Dear stranger, will you write me a poem
of stardust, sweet lust, melancholy memories?

I am made of that strand of moonlight
which descends on new moon nights
and lights a fire of unwieldy obsession
in ocean waves, love pangs, and lunatics.

I am that curve in the arrow of time,
the minuscule now, all of your yesterdays,
and as space, I churn far across the aeons,
burning pages of a book written without us.

Your Gifts

I asked for glass bangles of your love
to sing of nights that didn't want to end,
for green sarees of jasmine stalks
to wrap delicious memories of your eyes.
But you brought me gifts beyond the world,
a sacred scent of rain meeting parched earth,
and dark vermillion on our parted paths.

Lonely

Love, the loneliest of all words, comes and goes,
neither completing the slow kill it is mandated to do
nor bathing me in mists of moments I dreamed up
lying there under the stars, holding your hand
minute after minute; it pours hot coals of thwarted trust,
laughs at the heaven's sacred stardust, my vermillion dusk

Two Cups of Tea

My words flirt with your fingers,
memories embrace from behind
as watermarks on glass tabletops,
sunlight pours through clasped hands
and dries those fragrant keepsakes
for a day when you lie with your book
and think of two cups of tea
and a sunset at home.

The Parting

Goodbye

And so along comes goodbye to say hello to our souls.
Such a long journey from one lifetime to another—
all we could gather were a bundle of moments.
Here, take my share, move on, be happy again.
I will nurse my goodbyes in sunsets again.

Sorry, no sorry

No "sorry" for the lost time, that palace where hurt lives;
no "sorry" for today, just tomorrow's yesterday.
I apologize for not being, for being, for not seeing what I saw,
for existing, for living, for wanting, for crying,
for understanding what I could.
No "sorry" for mothers giving birth to daily hope,
and none at all for being left alone with no hope.
I give you no "sorry" for those evenings,
those dances on time's butterfly flippers,
lust's death-laden whispers; but oh, his life-giving chants!
No "sorry" for kisses, wild fumbles on Mars.
No "sorry" for crickets and wet cigarette butts.
No "sorry" for drunken nights, stars in broad daylight,
caskets of familiar lies, shards of broken trust.
No "sorry" for goodbye and farewell, sweet friend.

Pale Blue Dot

Maybe all these filters, bulbs, wires,
are really not enough, and maybe it
takes nothing but sheer darkness
to truly silhouette light.

Maybe all the love in the world erases no pain
from pockets of emptiness clipped onto
laundry lines behind our house, onto your hands,
those songs, that golden fuzzy glow.

Nights and days, inside and about, you and I—
I remember how we ruled the world,
but maybe half of you and half of me
was never really good enough by then

to defy fates, see new roads, discard dreams,
and maybe butterflies have to die on the other side
of the pale blue dot before the ground beneath
our feet will shake, stir, and then, perhaps then,

maybe only then will we sit down to count those
photographs in our phones: museums, sarees,
coffee tumblers, ghee lamps, mothers, daughters,
and two pale blue parallel lines that spelled the end.

Until Then

Until then, I will roll myself up
into this blanket of words and phrases.
I will make friends with thoughts and dreams.
Until then, I will say to the stars
that they were unborn once, and that I
was born from them, once.
One day, the stars too will be gone;
some have, it seems, already died
but shine anyway as though
they were ghosts of my words and dreams
refusing to believe
in a death that spells silence.
Until then, there will be words,
more of these letters and spaces strung together
forcing meaning into sounds and wounds
And all of those in-between could-have-beens.
One day, I too will have no words.
Until then, though,
it's not lips but those silent warmth of the stars;
not words but whispers of my name;
not your arms but your skin that melts into mine;
your breath, at once mine and
not once evermore.
Until then, I shall imagine
glorious dreams to take to another star.

Missing Women

A thousand ships sailed one day;
a million monkeys died on another—
because, you women, you were missed.

A silent night launches a secret sigh;
one hundred moons cry in a deep blue sky—
because, you woman, you aren't missed.

Who wrote those woman's stories?
Such glories that lead men to war!
What gripped your love so hard
as to be clipped by silence overall?

And yet,

Woman, who are you to ask of fate
why beauty dares yet to survive?
And why does it not die
when love fades and leaves us all?

Or Not

Perhaps when I see you again,
smiling your crinkled eyes into
near oblivion, I will ask you this.
Or not.

Does your pillow smell the way it did
When we laughed our way into it?
Tasting of fresh tangerines, seawater, and driftwood smoke,
skin on skin, lips adrift
in a sensuous sea of tangled senses?

Perhaps when I see you again,
I will see myself again in you, your fingers
entwined in mine, thoughts,
words, and memories
jumbling, tumbling.

Feet curled up against feet,
like dried flowers in forgotten books,
a hundred lifetimes clasped in a single night—
perhaps when I see you again
I will live again.
Or not.

Indira, You're Going to Be Here Tomorrow

Wondering if it was still worth
those coffees and bridges over rain,
breathless moons and silly limericks

I felt the urge to hold on and not
ever let go of him who
melted all too soon into the crowd.

But what of those afternoons
that linger as fragrant dried roses
somewhere in his everyday words?

You will still be tomorrow, Indira,
here to count moles on his beloved
half-forgotten face.

A Pact with Loneliness

A staircase running up to yesterday's clouds.
It is your crisp-starched shirt, smell of earth,
a killer whale torturing slow hours to death,
gnawing at my tired limbs and shredding
memory's flesh from the bone of ecstasy.

Loneliness draws parallel lines and laughs
in the face of my confused forays into
bookshops, moonlit sidewalks,
strangers' smiles, full shopping bags
on Saturday markets.

She whispered dreamy words
of tenderness and signed
a pact of honour.
I was to go wherever she did,
and she was to never leave me alone.

Time - Wrapped Desire

As heavens open their floodgates,
gushing forth in a thunderous frenzy,
do they still hug this very ground?
Kissing it fluid, languid, and volatile?

And when the afternoon's sun lost
its track, did he splash
lengthy shadows, half-yellow, half-crimson,
into unseen nooks and corners
of your mind and mine?

Watching this play of heaven and earth,
every pore of my being alive and alert
to mirth and madness,
I look around for you in our half-lit room.

What power do words have
that you pour your out soul, bent
over those books?
What price would I not pay
to partake of that stolen time?

Moment by moment, when the flood
trickled down,
grey clouds of desire lightened into
cotton whiffs of memories.

Did you ever wonder that had you kept the book down,
those words would not be sad and lonesome?
Or did you worry they would skip and run,
and like these shadows, turn and never return?

I see sometimes that this time and space have curved around
a place of yester-tomorrow,
but does a day truly turn onto itself,
devouring its tail,
that curved eternity of the null?

Or does time go on, and with it desire,
beyond null, beyond one?

You Will Be

You will be that hole in me which devours
every ray of hope shining through another window,
that hole into which I shed this burden of light,
of wanting to live, to know, and to see.

You will be that pain which I want to
find again and again in scabs of memories,
ripping through these mounds of unhealed
moments, those concrete mountains of lust.

Deeper and deeper I dig for some meaning.
It must have been as it was meant to be.
He must have left as he needed to find himself.
I must have been harsher than I ever wanted to.

They must have meant what they never said.
One day from another day I know
no difference anymore. Just as though
I still hold your fingers in my palm,

looking through the window into gushing
monsoons of the past,
those days which will never be back, those nights
which will never forget,

you will be the kaleidoscope that failed to
lure your future into our past—
and yet a yellow scarf lies somewhere
still untouched, unripped.

You will be the hand that brushed it aside
and walked out into your wide fields of joy,
closing in on me, my black hole, my love,
one atom at a time, all of world's windows.

The Calm After

Ganga's Lover

Ganga flows as though she were time
rushing to meet her lover for the era,
He of the blue throat dancing his mirthful destruction.
But alone, at unknown bends, she crashes
into blind terrains, unlit forests, and unforgiving cities.
I met you on her bank a whole lifetime ago.
Those crickets, like gentle thrusts of anklets,
strummed seasonal fingers on naked hormones.
I spoke then of want, of need, of voids and valleys,
while your deep full river flood of a kiss
crashed and tore, bent and danced on unlit
corners of my soul—where you and I
were born as a singularity—
and then wilfully flowed.
Until we meet yet again on the
far shores of the ocean of dissolution,
the Ganga flows, as though she were time.

Doubt and Hope

Twin peaks of infinite thirst
moulded by ancient, forgotten gods,
doubt and hope keep watch on life
and, like dawn and dusk,
relate to neither time nor space.

Millions of gods have been crushed
when heavens churned and roads
leading up to those peaks perished.
Uncounted pennies have been minted,
one day's loot, just enough for the next,

treasures, pleasures, lives gained
in the inner sanctum of one or the other.
At times one is lost in cloud shadows
of past lives and an unrepentant present
or in mystic mountain sunsets. But always
doubt and hope, like thought and word,
remain as heavy paperweights do,
keeping together the unwritten pages of
life's pointless lengthy short tales:
your story and mine, together or alone.

Again

Another truth, an alternate view,
an epiphany to save your life,
a new abacus to count blessings,
this ancient way to hold your breath,
that drive to practice, to compete, to win—

again this world will sell us
magic, hope, and dissent to dissipate
the nature, nay, the very soul of fear.
How many TED Talks does it take
to know what's known is known too late?

Why the Tortoise Got Its Shell

Since the time a mountain
was eased onto
my philanthropic back,
I turned a nomad.

Home is where I am alive,
and so I carry my heart, my beak,
eyes, innards, skin, and soul
so no hopes nor fears are left behind.

Home is somewhere to hide
my fingers bruised
from when I touched the fire
of your cardinal desire;

a legacy that will live on in
brooches and necklaces,
combs, hairpins, frames for eyeglasses,
delicate works of *bekko* art;

a sour old man's curse, this home, mine
to wear as a wedding present that never arrived,
weighing down on my need to roam,
to not run in the race—oh, to be a nomad!

Of Ancient Tales

Yes, Ships Do Dance!

Then this myth of an ancient ship
hauled alone by a prescient fish
sprawled on waves of a drowned wish.
They say I'd made an ordained trip.

I took seeds from Darwin's stingy grip,
sealed words from tomes of his niche,
packed wee wounds on my soul, amiss.
They say I sang of a future in worship.

But what is tomorrow if not an infant of the now—
cradled, cajoled from rivers of collective past
into delicious torrents of expectant trance?

They say today has been in a quantum vow
entangled in every ship's mission to last
until the fish learn to fly, or maybe to dance.

Memory

When the flame of hope flickers,
I visit you veiled
in shattered apparitions,
dulled, aching, distant, and serene.
Meaning and query are muddled
with reveries, desires, and quests.
I see my life as though it weren't mine.

In the sunlight of my everyday ambition,
you are but a memory of a lost time.

I dream of you and your smile,
and once again in the fissures of feelings,
those embers glisten and come to life.
I stand watching life shake itself
of ennui and listlessness
and embark on a slow jog into
concentric longings, needs, and wants.

Mount Fuji

Do you know of gods churning an ancient white ocean,
burying cauldrons of grief-tinged devotion
beneath this giant of a peakless mountain?

Do you know of days burning with reason or rhyme?
Or of those who truly know the poetry of time?
Did you hear those lies which mothers sing
of folk tales, sweet loves, and springtime?

One such tale they wove of him, a god who was born
when that unlikely couple met at a promiscuous dawn.
Tender earth made love to the mystical sky,
and they said he was born tiny, a tad too shy.

Along came grief, vanity, or jealous might.
He grew by the day and through the night.
His heart opened a longing hole heavenwards,
and his arms spilled over the earth downwards.

Perhaps he yearned to make a home for three
in misty cloud-cysts; his earth and his sky, never free.

His unborn brothers lie buried round his girth.
Who saw his birth? Who knew this worth?

He, Fujisan, sings their songs from autumn's lengthy tomes.
He, Fujisan, weaves clouds on his untracked mighty stones.

And down below we weave our punctured lives
into blurred portraits, false tales of truthful strife.

Fujisan, do you live in those stories of daily deaths,
of your mother's infinite thirst, her never-ending quest?

Waiting for Water

You queue up for water at ungodly
hours in a city of imagined ladders,
plastic tumblers of every hue
your passports to technicolour dreams.
Around the corner, they sew sinews
and nerves to cinema screens,
winged unicorns devour grown-ups,
But you wait your turn to be carried by chance.

You—you are just one among a billion
taught in Telugu to long, to not wait,
to belong in and around
temporary queues for temporary wants.

Airports feature in your dreams too—
oh yes, as bright as a hundred drums of
drinking water, freedom, being adult.
One hundred drums, twenty trumpets, and
fifty tall elephants in a temple fair, a queue to enter
every unopened door, jostling through
multitudes, senses, smells, desires—
all merged into a jealous, nervous wait for your turn.

Not too long after, the gods carry you on a crystal craft
to a mirror-wedged city
of perfectly aligned rubbish bins,
polite traffic lines, neat lunch queues.

You see small gaping holes in the sky.
You count them all, oozing technicoloured
airplane fuel, oil slicks from up the heavens,
stardust of memories, water gushing
from unlimited taps. Those holes in the sky
fill every cell of your mirror-wedged city.

And you learn to queue again
for toilet rolls, oil, and rice, and to seal
some of those holes but without
water this time around.

Karma's Capricious Land

Hang on; hold on to hope's longhand.
Smile your way into karma's capricious land.

Macaronic moral fables, these maddening mortal lies:
they claim you were born once; mountains and oceans too.
The universe, they say, was never here—who knew?

You live a day, you live a night, but seasons, years—
imperfect circles those, drawn in invisible tears

of a blue planet counting its aeons to null,
spinning to death, no moment too dull.

So I say, hold on to hope's longhand.
Smile your way into karma's capricious land.

The heavens today hold secrets of your tomorrows and yesterdays.
An arrowhead of crushed iron dispersed the blue god's haze.
This hunter and his hunted are both but one: time.
He sang of love, death, rebirth, and all within.
One tiny moment your eyes held mine, and therein

I said, hold on to hope's longhand.
Smile your way into karma's capricious land.

The Ganges descending from your lips, these heavens—
ah, such death I sought from nowhere, but you,
tangerine, layered in nectar, your embrace,
my words, swaying to your pulse, this dance …
ah, such life I craved from no one but you.
Tiny tributes to eternity, our tumbled kisses—

in them, I hold on to hope's longhand
and smile my way into karma's capricious land.

CPSIA information can be obtained
at www.ICGtesting.com
Printed in the USA
LVHW040345280423
745466LV00001B/8

9 781543 770568